Scored for Listening:
A Guide to Music

Second Edition

Scored for Listening:
A Guide to Music

Second Edition

Guy Alan Bockmon

William J. Starr

University of Tennessee

 Harcourt Brace Jovanovich, Inc.

New York   Chicago   San Francisco   Atlanta

Cover photo by Ken Weith from Shostal Associates, Inc.

Library of Congress Catalog Card Number: 79-183738

ISBN: 0-15-579055-2

Printed in the United States of America

ACKNOWLEDGMENTS

Permission to use copyright material is hereby gratefully acknowledged:

Boosey and Hawkes, Inc., for the first movement of *Concerto for Orchestra* by Béla Bartók, Copyright 1946 by Hawkes & Son (London) Ltd., reprinted by permission of Boosey and Hawkes, Inc.;
and for the second movement of *Octet for Wind Instruments* by Igor Stravinsky, Copyright 1924
by Edition Russe de Musique, renewed 1952. Copyright and renewal assigned to Boosey and
Hawkes, Inc. Revised version Copyright 1952 by Boosey and Hawkes, Inc. Reprinted by permission.

Universal Edition, Vienna, for the first movement of Webern's *Quartet for Violin, Clarinet, Tenor
Saxophone, and Piano, Op. 22,* Copyright 1932 by Universal Edition, Vienna. Used by permission
of the publisher. Theodore Presser Company sole representatives, U.S.A., Canada, and Mexico.

Preface

Since SCORED FOR LISTENING first appeared in 1959, the line score has proved itself as an invaluable teaching device in introductory music classes. Many thousands of students have discovered that they can readily learn to follow a line score and that doing so substitutes active participation for passive—and sometimes inattentive—listening, aids memory and understanding, and facilitates reference to specific passages in lectures and discussion.

This new edition of SCORED FOR LISTENING differs from its predecessors in several important respects. One of our principal aims has been to make the text less technical and more readable. The book now begins with a very brief introduction to the most basic terms the student will need in order to discuss the works to be studied and then proceeds immediately to the works themselves. These are presented chronologically, but they may be taken up in any order. Each line score is preceded by a brief, non-technical discussion of the style and form of the work and by a set of listening questions, answers to which are given in the back of the book; the questions provide the student with a way of checking his ability to hear what is happening in the music and remind him constantly that following the line scores is always a means to an end and not an end in itself.

In selecting the works to be represented in this edition, we have included what for us and our colleagues have been the most successful pieces in the original SCORED FOR LISTENING and its companion Alternate Edition. To these we have added a number of new works, particularly with a view to giving greater representation to the music of the twentieth century. As in the earlier books, the emphasis is on whole works or whole movements of long works. In the present book, however, all works (with three exceptions, explained in their introductions) are given in line score or full score; several works shown in abbreviated form in the earlier books have been expanded to continuous line score. The final work in the book offers an opportunity for a little active music-making as it makes its point about the aleatoric nature of some modern music. If it inspires classes to further creative explorations of sound, so much the better.

A set of six stereo recordings containing all of the selections in the book (except, obviously, for the *Concerto for Classroom Impromptu*) is available from the publisher.

We should like to express our appreciation to Professor Harry B. Lincoln of the State University of New York at Binghamton, who read the entire manuscript of the new edition and made a number of helpful suggestions.

GAB

WJS

Contents

Scored for Listening:
A Guide to Music

Second Edition

Introduction
Toward a Musical
Vocabulary

Music is made of sounds and silences. Some works are committed by the composer to a *score*, a written notation of the sounds and silences to be interpreted and realized by a performer. Others are *improvised* by the composer, who performs the music as he composes it; others have sections to be improvised by the performer. Still others are recorded by the composer directly on magnetic tape. And several of these approaches may be combined in a single work.

The sounds of which music is made possess three characteristics: *volume*, perceived as "loud" or "soft"; *quality*, which enables the listener to distinguish between sounds produced by different sources; and *duration*, or length of the sound in time. Many sounds also have definite *pitch*, perceived as "high" or "low," while others do not.

Volume

Volume is used in music in relatively simple ways. In the score the composer's directions to the performer about *dynamics* (levels of volume) are shown by the initial letters of the Italian words *forte* (loud), *piano* (soft), and *mezzo* (moderately). Used in combination, they can indicate a scale of dynamics from softest possible to loudest possible: *pppp, ppp, pp, p, mp, mf, f, ff, fff, ffff*.

Gradual changes in dynamic level are indicated by *crescendo* (increasing intensity) and *diminuendo* (decreasing intensity) or by their abbreviations, *cresc.* and *dim.* They are also indicated by their respective symbols:

1

Quality

The quality of sound is the physical basis for *tone color* in music. Individual voices or instruments are relatively limited in color, but in combinations they provide almost unlimited resources of tone color.

Singing, which originated as an intensification of speech, is perhaps the oldest medium of musical expression. Singing was so important in the development of music that the instruments of the orchestra are grouped in sections called *choirs*, and the strands of melody they play are sometimes called *voices*. The basic choral group is the SATB (abbreviations for *soprano, alto, tenor, bass*) chorus like that used in the "Crucifixus" (pp. 36–39) by Johann Sebastian Bach.

An introduction to the sounds of the instruments of the orchestra is to be found in Benjamin Britten's *Young Person's Guide to the Orchestra* (p. 204).

Duration

The relative durations of sounds and silences within the framework of a piece of music are the principal creators of *rhythm*. The durations of sounds as they are notated in a score are somewhat affected by modes of attack and release, which may be *staccato* (short and disconnected), *legato* (connected without perceptible pause) or somewhere between. They may also be affected by *accent* (special stress, weight, or emphasis given to a particular note).

There are two fundamental kinds of rhythm in music, *metrical* rhythm, or rhythm that involves *meter* (measure), and *nonmetrical* rhythm, which does not involve meter. Nonmetrical rhythm can be heard in the Gregorian chant (p. 11) and is akin to the rhythm of prose or blank verse. There are longer and shorter durations and there are accents, but there is no regularly recurring pattern of accents as there is in a piece that has meter.

Metrical rhythm can be heard in the second movement of Franz Joseph Haydn's *Symphony No. 94* (pp. 70–72), in which the patterns of sounds and silences are superimposed on a background of *beats* (audible or inferred pulses that measure elapsed time), which are organized into pairs. The score is marked off by vertical *bar lines* into *measures* of two beats each. Henry Purcell's "Lament" from his *Dido and Aeneas* (pp. 17–19) also has metrical rhythm, but the beats are grouped in threes, each measure consisting of one group of three beats.

The Purcell piece and Britten's *Young Person's Guide to the Orchestra* are organized identically from the standpoint of meter. One important difference between them is a difference of *tempo*. The Italian word *tempo* means "time," but it has come to have a narrower meaning to musicians: the frequency of beats as they occur in time. The tempo of the Britten piece is faster than the tempo of Purcell's.

In many scores, the tempo is given as a number of beats per minute; in others, Italian words are used to indicate the approximate tempo. The basic terms, in order from slowest to fastest, are *grave, largo, adagio, moderato, andante, allegro, vivace,* and *presto.*

In poetry, metrical feet are combined to form lines of verse; in music, metrical units are combined to form larger structures called *phrases.* Phrases are concluded by musical effects of punctuation called *cadences,* which, like punctuation in writing, can be either inconclusive, like a comma or a question mark, or conclusive, like a period or an exclamation point.

Pitch

As we hear pitches occur in a piece of music, we tend to organize them in one or more of three ways: *melodically, contrapuntally,* and *harmonically.* If we hear successive pitches related to each other so that each seems to derive from those that precede it and to lead into those that follow, we are listening melodically and hear a *melodic line.* If we hear two or more melodic lines combined at the same time, as in the Palestrina work (pp. 13–14), we are hearing the melodies in *counterpoint,* or contrapuntally. If we hear simultaneous "stacks" of pitches combined with each other and progressing to and from each other, we are hearing *harmonically,* with our attention on *chords,* as in the introduction to the second movement of Antonin Dvořák's symphony (pp. 168–69).

When we are hearing melodically, we are aware of *contour,* the rise and fall of the melodic line. Some melodies move step by step up and down the *scale* (from the Italian *scala,* "ladder") with an occasional *leap* (skipping a few ladder rungs) for the sake of variety. Other melodies make frequent wide leaps, especially in instrumental music. The texture of music that consists purely of melody, such as Gregorian chant (p. 11), is *monophonic.*

When we are hearing a *polyphonic* texture contrapuntally, we are aware of the contours of the participating melodies and of the degrees of *consonance* and *dissonance* between them as dissonant notes clash with each other and resolve into consonance. In Bach's "Crucifixus" the first note in each measure from measure 6 through measure 13 in the choral score (p. 36) is dissonant and is followed by consonance. When we listen harmonically, we are aware of *key* and *tonality* (except in styles in which key and tonality are absent) when we hear chords related to each other and to one chord of special significance. Tonality is hard to understand but easy to experience. Listeners who could not begin to describe tonality can hear it. Careful listening to the first four measures of the Haydn movement (p. 70) will reveal that one chord occurs in the first two measures, a second chord in the third measure, and a third chord in the fourth measure. The effect of the second chord is to predict the third, and the effect of the third chord is to predict the return to the first. The predictability of chord progression, unknown in non-Western music, may be a matter of conditioning. The listener who has experienced this relationship between these three chords has experienced tonality, the gravitation toward a reappearance of the initial chord, and has experienced something about the key of C major, because the initial chord in the progression is a C major chord. Compare these measures with what happens harmonically in measures 49–52, in which the tonality is the same but the focus is on a C minor chord, creating the key of C minor.

In much of the music we hear, we find ourselves listening melodically, contrapuntally, and harmonically all at the same time. In measures 82–105 of the Haydn movement, we hear the melody in the violins, a second melody played by the woodwinds, and the harmony provided by their momentary combinations of pitches.

Musical Ideas

Musical ideas are memorable relationships among sounds. They may concern particular effects of tone color, striking harmonic sonorities or progressions, relationships between tonalities, or some other organization of sounds. In many pieces the ideas are presented as patterns of rhythm and melody, the simplest and shortest of which is called a *motive*. The motive with which Beethoven's Fifth Symphony (p. 85) begins features a rhythmic idea of four notes, short-short-short-long. It is heard hundreds of times in the piece. Longer musical ideas called *themes* or *subjects* are made from statements and reiterations of motives, as is the first theme of the Beethoven symphony.

Melodic ideas are expanded into themes and into extended works by such devices as *repetition, sequence, imitation,* and *transformation.*

Repetition of an idea in the same voice (whether a human voice or any instrumental voice) at the same pitch is the simplest and most obvious means of expansion, common in children's songs and in primitive chants. In measures 14–17 of the first movement of the Beethoven symphony (p. 85), a four-note idea is stated in the first violins and repeated exactly.

Sequence involves the same idea in the same voice at a different pitch. In measures 75–82 of the Beethoven movement, the first violins take up a four-measure idea and then play the idea at a higher pitch, creating a sequence.

Imitation takes up an idea (or some recognizable form of it) in a different voice at the same pitch or at a different pitch. Listen to the following examples in the Beethoven symphony. In measures 63–74, the violins state a four-measure idea, which is imitated immediately by the clarinet and then by the flute. In measures 14–17, the four-note idea of the first violins is imitated by the second violins by *inversion* of the contour of the idea, so that the line moves upward rather than downward. In the third movement, the low strings state an idea beginning in measure 140 that is imitated, in turn, by the violas, the second violins, and the first violins.

Transformation is difficult to identify by hearing, because the connection between the statement of an idea and its recurrent form is tenuous. For instance, in measures 63–78 of the Beethoven first movement there are four melodic fragments. Can you detect a relationship between the highest pitch in each and the initial motive of the piece?

Devices for the systematic variation of rhythmic patterns include *augmentation* and *diminution*, which involve respectively the lengthening and shortening of durations, usually by double and half. Augmentation can be heard clearly in the second movement of Dvořák's ninth symphony (p. 168) as the material of measure 19 is stretched, or augmented, to make measures 20–21. Diminution is prominent in the fourth movement of the same symphony in the measures following the appearance of Theme I at measure 140.

Variation and Development

The techniques of variation and development are in some ways similar but there is a basic difference. The composer's goal in a form based on variation, like the second movement of Haydn's *Symphony No. 94* (pp. 70–72), is to state his theme and then to compose variations on that theme, the theme itself staying more or less intact. The goal in development is to state a theme and then explore its possibilities. Beethoven, in the first movement of the *Fifth Symphony*, for instance, picked a little fragment (measures 60–61) of his second theme and proceeded to develop that two-note idea for fourteen measures, and then he continued to develop what seems to be one of the two notes.

Forms

As a musical work is performed, the perceptive listener hears, in addition to momentary detail, such things as the proportions of the phrases, the order of presentation of musical ideas, the expansions and derivations of those ideas, and the relationship of the various parts to the whole.

In many traditional works, these matters of proportion, order, expansion, derivation, and relationship are arranged in accordance with the scheme of one or another of the musical *forms*, esthetically satisfactory designs to which some works adhere precisely, some only in principle, and others not at all.

The traditional forms fall into two broad categories: works that are self-contained and independent, comparable to a book in one volume, and extended works composed of two or more self-contained but interdependent *numbers* (in most vocal music) or *movements* (in most instrumental music), which are comparable to individual volumes in a book of more than one volume.

Notation

To follow the scores, reduced scores, and one-line scores in this book, it is not necessary to be able to read music. All that is needed is to understand that the higher the notes sound, the higher they appear to be in print; the lower they sound, the lower they are in print. Also, the blacker the notes are, the faster they go, and the whiter they are, the slower they go.

The exceptions occur when a change is made from the treble clef to the bass clef or vice versa—as in the first movement of Beethoven's *Symphony No. 5* in measure 28 (treble to bass) and measure 29 (bass to treble), when the apparent direction of the line is affected by the clef change—and when the durations of notes and rests are affected by changes in meter or tempo or both, as occurs when the blacker notes of Beethoven's second movement sound slower than the whiter notes of the first movement.

Gregorian Chant

Mass for Weekdays in Advent and Lent

During the sixth century A.D., Pope Gregory the Great collected and codified the music of the Roman Catholic Church, which had developed from ancient Hebrew, Greek, Armenian, Syrian, and Byzantine music. The vast quantities of *plainsong* codified by Gregory, and thus called *Gregorian chant*, and other chants added later constitute the most important examples of music surviving from the first thousand years of the Christian era.

Plainsong refers to unmetrical compositions with monophonic texture. Typically, the melodic motions are small, mostly by step with a few narrow leaps. The range of pitch is severely restricted, the contour is smooth, and the rhythm, strongly influenced by the accentual and durational rhythm of the text, is unhurried and free, devoid of heavy accents.

The most common musical settings of the Mass, the solemn service of the Roman Catholic Church, consist of the five sections that do not change during the year. The text of these, known together as the Ordinary of the Mass, follows:

KYRIE

(*Greek text*) Kyrie eleison. Christe eleison. Kyrie eleison.

Lord, have mercy on us. Christ, have mercy on us. Lord, have mercy on us.

GLORIA

(*Latin text*) Gloria in excelsis Deo. Et in terra pax hominibus bonae voluntatis. Laudamus te. Benedicimus te. Adoramus te. Glorificamus te. Gratias agimus tibi propter magnam gloriam tuam. Domine Deus, Rex coelestis, Deus Pater omnipotens. Domine Fili unigenite, Jesu Christe. Domine Deus, Agnus Dei, Filius Patris. Qui tollis peccata mundi, miserere nobis. Qui tollis peccata mundi, suscipe deprecationem nostram. Qui sedes ad dexteram Patris, miserere nobis. Quoniam tu solus sanctus. Tu solus Dominus. Tu solus altissimus, Jesu Christe, cum Sancto Spiritu, in gloria Dei Patris. Amen.

Glory be to God in the highest. And on earth peace to men of good will. We praise Thee. We bless Thee. We adore Thee. We glorify Thee. We give Thee thanks for Thy great glory. O Lord God, heavenly King, God the Father almighty. O Lord the only-begotten Son, Jesus Christ. O Lord God, lamb of God, Son of the Father. Thou who takest away the sins of the world, have mercy on us. Thou who takest away the sins of the world, receive our prayer. Thou who sittest at the right hand of the Father, have mercy on us. For Thou alone art holy. Thou alone art Lord. Thou alone, O Jesus Christ, art most high, together with the Holy Spirit, in the glory of God the Father. Amen.

7

CREDO

Credo in unum Deum, Patrem omnipotentem, factorem coeli et terrae, visibilium omnium, et invisibilium. Et in unum Dominum Jesum Christum, Filium Dei unigenitum, et ex Patre natum ante omnia saecula: Deum de Deo, lumen de lumine, Deum verum de Deo vero, genitum, non factum, consubstantialem Patri, per quem omnia facta sunt. Qui propter nos homines, et propter nostram salutem, descendit de coelis, et incarnatus est de Spiritu Sancto ex Maria Virgine, et homo factus est. Crucifixus etiam pro nobis, sub Pontio Pilato passus, et sepultus est. Et resurrexit tertia die, secundum Scripturas, et ascendit in coelum: sedet ad dexteram Patris. Et iterum venturus est, cum gloria, judicare vivos et mortuos, cujus regni non erit finis. Et in Spiritum Sanctum, Dominum et vivificantem, qui ex Patre Filioque procedit. Qui cum Patre et Filio simul adoratur et conglorificatur, qui locutus est per Prophetas. Et in unam sanctum catholicam et apostolicam Ecclesiam. Confiteor unum baptisma in remissionem peccatorum. Et expecto resurrectionem mortuorum. Et vitam venturi saeculi. Amen.

I believe in one God, the Father almighty, maker of heaven and earth, and of all things visible and invisible. And in one Lord Jesus Christ, the only-begotten Son of God, born of the Father before all ages: God of God, light of light, true God of true God, begotten, not made, of one being with the Father, by Whom all things were made. Who for us men, and for our salvation, came down from heaven, and was made flesh by the Holy Spirit of the Virgin Mary, and was made man. He also was crucified for us, suffered under Pontius Pilate, and was buried. And on the third day He rose again, according to the Scriptures, and ascended into heaven. He sitteth at the right hand of the Father. And He shall come again, with glory, to judge both the living and the dead, Whose kingdom shall have no end. And I believe in the Holy Spirit, Lord and giver of life, Who proceedeth from the Father and the Son, Who together with the Father and the Son is adored and glorified, Who spoke by the Prophets. And I believe in one holy catholic and apostolic Church. I confess one baptism for the remission of sins. And I look for the resurrection of the dead and the life of the world to come. Amen.

SANCTUS

Sanctus, Sanctus, Sanctus, Dominus Deus Sabaoth. Pleni sunt coeli et terra gloria tua. Hosanna in excelsis. Benedictus qui venit in nomine Domini. Hosanna in excelsis.

Holy, Holy, Holy, Lord God of hosts. Heaven and earth are filled with Thy glory. Hosanna in the highest. Blessed is He that cometh in the name of the Lord. Hosanna in the highest.

AGNUS DEI

Agnus Dei, qui tollis peccata mundi: miserere nobis. Agnus Dei, qui tollis peccata mundi: miserere nobis. Agnus Dei, qui tollis peccata mundi: dona nobis pacem.

Lamb of God, who takest away the sins of the world: have mercy on us. Lamb of God, who takest away the sins of the world: have mercy on us. Lamb of God, who takest away the sins of the world: grant us peace.

Questions for Self-Testing

1. In the "Sanctus" as sung in the Gregorian chant, five cadences are heard, coinciding with the periods that punctuate the Latin text. Which two fall on the lowest pitch?

   a. the first, at *Sabaoth*
   b. the second, at *tua*
   c. the third, at *excelsis*
   d. the fourth, at *Domini*
   e. the fifth, at *excelsis*

2. A melodic idea is introduced at "Sanctus, Dominus . . ." On what text do you hear that melodic idea return?

   a. *Deus Sabaoth*
   b. *gloria tua*
   c. *in nomine Domini*
   d. *Hosanna in excelsis*

3. All three phrases of the "Agnus Dei" end on the same pitch. In the text below, underscore each syllable on which you hear a cadence.

   Agnus Dei, qui tollis peccata mundi: miserere nobis.
   Agnus Dei, qui tollis peccata mundi: miserere nobis.
   Agnus Dei, qui tollis peccata mundi: dona nobis pacem.

4. At cadences in the "Agnus Dei" and in the "Sanctus," the same pitch is heard

   a. six of eight times
   b. three of eight times
   c. five of eight times

5. Each section of the "Agnus Dei" begins with

   a. the melodic idea from the beginning of the "Sanctus"
   b. a new musical idea
   c. a cadence

6. The text of the second section of the "Agnus Dei" is identical with that of the first. The musical setting is

    a. identical
    b. related, but not identical
    c. different

7. The text of the third section of the "Agnus Dei" begins like that of the first and second sections but ends differently. The musical setting of the third section is

    a. identical
    b. related, but not identical
    c. different

Gregorian Chant

Mass for Weekdays in Advent and Lent

Sanctus

Holy, Holy, Holy, Lord God of hosts. Heaven and earth are filled with Thy glory. Hosanna in the highest. Blessed is He that cometh in the name of the Lord. Hosanna in the highest.

Agnus Dei

Lamb of God, who takest away the sins of the world: have mercy on us. Lamb of God, who takest away the sins of the world: have mercy on us. Lamb of God, who takest away the sins of the world: grant us peace.

Giovanni Pierluigi da Palestrina

(1525–1594)

Adoramus te Christe

Palestrina was employed by the Catholic Church in Italy to compose Masses, motets, and other ceremonial music. In addition he wrote madrigals and other pieces for secular enjoyment. The brief motet *Adoramus te Christe* is a polyphonic choral work consisting of six sections, each devoted to a phrase of the sacred Latin text and set apart by a cadence. In some sections all voices sing the same words at the same time; in others, a rich interplay of accents is heard as words overlap between and among the four voices. Bar lines, used in modern editions for the convenience of the performers, were not used in the original editions, and the engaging rhythmic activity results, in part, from the interplays of two-beat and three-beat patterns as they conflict with each other.

The tempo is unchanging, the music being propelled by a steady pulse without heavy accents. Imitation is the most important means of expanding musical ideas in music of this period. The tenor in measures 11–13 is loosely imitated by the bass in measures 14–16, by the soprano in measures 15–16, and by the alto in measures 14–15; and the line begun by the alto and tenor in measure 19 is imitated immediately by the soprano and later (in measures 22–23) by the bass.

Questions for Self-Testing

1. Where are the cadences that separate the sections?

    measures _____ , _____ , _____ , _____ , and _____

2. The only cadences not bridged over by new activity in one or more voices are in measures _____ and _____ .

3. Section 5 consists of
    a. new material
    b. a return of the initial material
    c. a summary of sections 3 and 4

Giovanni Pierluigi da Palestrina

Adoramus te Christe: Motet (1581)

We adore Thee, O Christ, and we bless Thee, because by Thy cross Thou hast redeemed the world. Have mercy on us.

Henry Purcell

(c. 1659–1695)

Dido and Aeneas

Having attained by 1682 the position of "Composer in Ordinary to His Most Sacred Majesty and Organist of the Chapel Royal" at the court of Charles II of England, Purcell composed anthems, odes, chamber music, pieces for keyboard instruments, incidental music for plays, "welcome songs" for distinguished visitors, and the earliest English opera still in the repertory, *Dido and Aeneas*.

The excerpt given here consists of a *recitative*, a free vocal line that presents narrative and descriptive material in succinct fashion; an *aria*, an accompanied solo song; and a four-part chorus. The scene concludes the opera: Dido, who has been abandoned by Aeneas, has taken her life by falling on his sword and, dying, she sings the aria that is often called "Dido's Lament." The lament is based on a five-measure *basso ostinato* or *ground bass*, a phrase-length melody repeated several times while the solo voice and upper instruments spin out melodies and countermelodies. The small descending steps that are heard in the ostinato melody and between the fourth and fifth notes of the vocal solo establish the atmosphere of grief and tragedy by "sighing" in a way familiar to composers and audiences in the seventeenth century.

Questions for Self-Testing

1. The meter of the lament organizes the beats in

    a. pairs
    b. threes

2. At what two points do the ostinato and the solo voice cadence together?

    a. first double bar
    b. second double bar
    c. third double bar
    d. before last repeated section
    e. at the conclusion of the solo

3. The cadence where the solo voice ends is

    a. complete
    b. incomplete
    c. nonexistent

4. How many times is the basso ostinato heard?

    a. seven
    b. eleven
    c. seventeen

5. The text of the chorus is set in five sections, each terminated by a cadence. The cadences occur in measures _____ , _____ , _____ , _____ , and _____ .

6. In the first section, which word has the most emotional impact?
   _____

7. How does Purcell *text-paint* that word—that is, express the meaning musically?
   a. by dissonance in the harmony
   b. by contrast of soft with loud
   c. by descending melodic lines

8. Which word is given special prominence in the second section?
   _____

9. Which word is given special prominence in the third section?
   _____

Henry Purcell

Excerpt from *Dido and Aeneas* (*c.* 1690)

Recitative: Thy hand, Belinda; darkness shades me:
On thy bosom let me rest!
More I would, but Death invades me:
Death is now a welcome guest!

Johann Sebastian Bach
(1685–1750)

Brandenburg Concerto No. 2 in F Major

Before the eighteenth century, instrumental music had played only a secondary role, having been used to accompany singing and dancing and for ceremonial and military purposes. Early in the eighteenth century, however, music for instruments alone gained in importance as dance music became stylized as music for listening, rather than exclusively for dancing, and as *concerted* music, made by instruments playing together, found an audience.

Orchestras came into being at royal courts. The instrumentation, which was not standardized, included flutes, oboes, bassoons, and strings plus *continuo*. The continuo is a combination of a keyboard instrument (usually a harpsichord) and a bass instrument (usually a cello) that performs the *figured bass*, a continuous written-out bass part with figures (numbers) representing the harmonies to be improvised by the keyboard performer (who frequently was the composer).

The second Brandenburg concerto is one of six dedicated to the Margrave of Brandenburg in 1721, at which time Bach was in the service of Prince Leopold of Anhalt-Cöthen, composing for and conducting the court orchestra. That the prince was one of the players in the orchestra speaks of his interest in music and in his orchestra.

As eighteenth-century composers grappled with problems of form and procedure in instrumental music, one of the forms that emerged and became prominent was the *concerto grosso*. The basic principle in the concerto grosso is the contrast between a small group of instruments, treated as a solo unit, and a larger group of instruments.

In the second Brandenburg concerto, the *concertino* (the small, soloistic group) consists of an unusual combination of instruments: the brilliant "Baroque trumpet" (the pitch of which is several degrees higher than that of a standard modern trumpet), a recorder (a flute-like instrument), an oboe, and a violin. The *ripieno* (large group) consists of strings and continuo. The three movements in fast-slow-fast order are typical of the concerto grosso.

Questions for Self-Testing

1. The two devices featured in measures 32–35 of the first movement are
    a. repetition
    b. imitation
    c. sequence
    d. inversion

2. Measures 11–12 are related to measures 1–2 by
    a. repetition
    b. imitation
    c. sequence
    d. inversion

3. Measures 19–20 are related to measures 1–2 by
    a. repetition
    b. imitation
    c. sequence
    d. inversion

4. In measures 60–67, the *concertino* instruments make their entrances
    a. in imitation
    b. as a basso continuo
    c. together

5. Two elements conspicuously omitted from the second movement are
    a. *ripieno*
    b. continuo
    c. trumpet
    d. flute

6. The device most important in the second movement is
    a. repetition
    b. imitation
    c. sequence
    d. inversion

7. The third movement begins with a 32–measure section featuring
    a. basso ostinato
    b. imitation
    c. an aria

8. The rhythm played by the trumpet in measures 7–9 is heard in measures 21–23 played by _____, in measures 30–32 played by _____, in measures 41–43 played by _____, in measures 44–46 played by _____, and in measures 47–52 when, for the first time in this movement, we hear the
    a. continuo
    b. *concertino*
    c. *ripieno*

9. After its prominent role in measures 72–88, the *continuo* plays, in measures 80–84
    a. a long, sustained tone
    b. the rhythm considered in the question above
    c. a series of descending sequences

Johann Sebastian Bach

Brandenburg Concerto No. 2 in F Major (1721)

First Movement

trumpet, oboe alternate

violins

oboe

violin

trumpet

soloists alternate

trumpet

flute, trumpet alternate

flute, violin alternate

orch.

oboe

flute

violin

oboe

flute

trumpet

orch.

Second Movement

Third Movement

Johann Sebastian Bach

(1685–1750)

Fugue in C Minor from *The Well-Tempered Clavier, Vol. I,
No. 2*

Each of the two volumes of *The Well-Tempered Clavier* consists of twenty-four
preludes and fugues, one in each of the twenty-four major and minor keys.
Designed as instructional material for students of keyboard playing, these pieces
have been used for this purpose for generations, but because of their musicality
they are also performed as recital pieces. Some of them, including this fugue,
have such an infectious, jazzy rhythm that they have become popular as performed by a choral group backed by drums and bass.

The *fugue* is a form based on imitation. It consists of *expositions* of the
subject (the theme) and *answers* (imitations of the subject) separated by *episodes*,
in which the subject is not present in its entirety. Answers may be *real* (an exact
duplicate of the contour of the subject, although it may begin at a different pitch)
or *tonal* (maintaining the basic shape of the contour of the subject but with slight
alterations).

Questions for Self-Testing

1. There are three equally important and equally prominent melodic lines
   (voices) in this polyphonic texture. In which voice is the subject announced?

   a. highest
   b. middle
   c. lowest

2. The characteristic rhythm of the first five notes of the subject is absent
   from measures

   a. 5–6
   b. 9–10
   c. 13–14
   d. 17–19
   e. 24

3. Halfway through measure 29 we hear

   a. the first complete cadence in the piece
   b. the beginning of a *codetta* (miniature coda)
   c. a long, sustained note begun in the bass

4. The answer beginning in measure 15 is

   a. real
   b. tonal

Johann Sebastian Bach

Fugue in C Minor from *The Well Tempered Clavier, Vol. I, No. 2* (1722)

Johann Sebastian Bach
(1685–1750)

Mass in B Minor

Composed during Bach's later years while he was Cantor at St. Thomas School in Leipzig and director of music in several local churches, the B minor Mass is a monumental work consisting of twenty-four movements. Because of its length—it requires several hours to perform—the work is not useful as music for church services. It is instead a concert Mass.

The "Crucifixus," a setting of a portion of the text from the *Credo,* is one of several movements for which Bach borrowed some of the music from one of his earlier cantatas, Passions, and other choral works, of which he had composed hundreds for special occasions in the Church year.

Built over a four-measure basso ostinato (compare it with that in the excerpt from *Dido and Aeneas,* page 17), the grief-stricken aura of the movement is pointed out by the "Baroque sigh" heard on the third syllable of the text sung by the sopranos. This falling figure recurs repeatedly throughout the movement. Bach's sensitive handling of text is dramatically demonstrated by the contrast in the opening of the "Et resurrexit" ("And He rose again on the third day according to the Scriptures"), which immediately follows the "Crucifixus."

Questions for Self-Testing

1. How many times is the four-measure ostinato heard? _____

2. In what measure does the contour of the ostinato change for the first time? _____

3. The first cadence not bridged over by continuing rhythmic activity comes just before the words _____ .

4. What keyboard instrument is used in the continuo in the recording you are using? _____

5. The voices begin with ten overlapping entrances on the word *crucifixus.* In what way are the second four entrances related to the first four?

    a. different voices on same notes
    b. by inversion
    c. by sequence

Johann Sebastian Bach

"Crucifixus" from *Mass in B Minor* (1738)

He was crucified for us under Pontius Pilate, suffered and was buried.

Wolfgang Amadeus Mozart
(1756–1791)

The Marriage of Figaro

Throughout the history of composed music run two esthetic codes, *classicism* and *romanticism,* one usually figuring more prominently than the other at a given time. In classicism, which favors stability, clarity, symmetry, and conformity to tradition and established practices, content must be adapted to the restraints of form, the manner of expression being as important as the thought to be expressed. Classic art is expressive but in the objective manner of a more or less disinterested observer rather than in the subjective manner of one who is personally involved.

There have been several periods in the history of music during which classic thought prevailed. The capitalized word "Classic," however, is usually applied to the period beginning about 1750 and extending into the early part of the nineteenth century.

The sound of the music of the period is light and relatively transparent; voices and instruments sound in their medium-high and medium-low registers, avoiding the brilliance and density of the extreme ranges. The rhythm is simple and regular, and there are infrequent changes of tempo within a movement. The important melodies are usually heard in the highest voice, which is supported by a rather simple harmonic accompaniment and is sometimes heard with a contrasting countermelody.

A basic feature of the style is the contrast of keys; one key is established at the beginning of a piece, others are explored in the middle, and the original key is reintroduced at the end. The proportions of the forms are usually clearly defined by musical punctuation. Phrases are generally short, clear, and regular, and cadences are frequent, strongly establishing tonalities.

From his first opera, *La Finta Semplice,* composed when he was twelve years old, to *The Magic Flute,* composed in the year of his death, Mozart was a prolific composer of operas. During the latter part of the eighteenth century, performances of purely instrumental music were still largely limited to the ruling class, but Italian opera had become immensely popular, drawing large and enthusiastic admissions-paying audiences to the opera houses of the cities of Europe.

The Marriage of Figaro was completed on April 29, 1786, and was given its first performance in Vienna two days later, a chronology that suggests that the company must have rehearsed the first act from scores on which the ink was not quite dry while the composer was working on the following acts.

Questions for Self-Testing

1. Between the three numbers in this excerpt there are *secco recitatives.* Determine by listening which best describes a *secco* recitative:

a. there is no instrumental accompaniment
b. the instrumental accompaniment dramatically reflects the meaning of the text
c. the instrumental accompaniment consists of a few punctuating and supporting chords

2. The idea begun in measure 9 is expanded by

    a. sequences of a fragment of the idea
    b. repetition with change of instruments
    c. augmentation of a rhythmic motive

3. The material of the first seven measures recurs in measures 18–26, expanded to nine measures by

    a. augmentation
    b. additional repeated notes
    c. additional new material

Wolfgang Amadeus Mozart

The Marriage of Figaro (1786)

From Act I

The plot of the opera revolves about the intrigues of Count Almaviva with Susanna, the Countess's maid. The Count's valet, Figaro, who is about to be married to Susanna, discovers that she is the object of the Count's affections, and Figaro is determined to use his wits to thwart him.

As the first scene opens, Figaro is seen measuring the floor of a partially furnished room, while Susanna, before a mirror, tries on a hat.

No. 1   Duet: Figaro and Susanna. (English translation on p. 50.)

In the *secco* recitative that follows, Susanna inquires of Figaro why he is measuring the room. Figaro replies that he is trying to discover the best place in the room for the bed the Count has given them as a wedding present. Susanna protests that she does not want this room; she has reasons that he does not know about. Figaro cannot understand why she will not have it, as it is the best room of the palace.

No. 2   Duet: Figaro and Susanna. (English translation on p. 50.)

In the next dialogue, in *secco* recitative, Susanna discloses to Figaro that the Count has eyes for none other than his little Susanna. For this reason, she says, he has given them this room, and her a handsome dowry. Figaro is incredulous. At this moment the Countess's bell rings, and Susanna leaves the room. Figaro then begins to awaken to the Count's purpose, and he vows that his plans shall not succeed.

No. 3   Aria: Figaro. (English translation on p. 51.)

le suo - ne - rò, si,   le suo-ne-rò, si,   le suo-ne-rò.

Se vuol ve - ni - re   nel-la mia sco-la,   la ca - pri - o - la

le in-se-gne - rò,   se vuol ve - ni - re   nel-la mia sco-la,   la ca - pri -

-o - la   le in - se -gne-rò, si,   le in - se-gne - rò, si,   le in - se-gne -

- rò.   Sa -prò,   sa-

violins

-prò,   sa - prò   sa - prò   sa -

violins

prò   ma pia - no,   pia-no, pia - no,

pia - no, pia - no, pia - no,   pia - no,

violins

me-gl'ogni arca-no dis-si-mu-lan-do sco-prir po-trò.   *Presto*   L'ar-te scher-

- men-do, l'ar-te a-do-pran-do,   di qua pun-gnen-do, di la scher-zan-do,   tut - te le

macchine ro -ve-scie-rò, ro - ve - scie - rò.   L'ar-te scher-

-men-do, l'ar - te a-do-pran-do,   di qua pun-gnen-do, di   là scher-zan-do,   tut - te le

No. 1   Duet

FIGARO: Five, ten, twenty, thirty, thirty-six, forty-three.
SUSANNA: Yes, I am truly contented, it seems in truth just made for me.
Please look here, my dearest Figaro, look one moment at my hat.
FIGARO: Yes, my love, it is very beautiful, seems in truth just made for you.

SUSANNA and } Ah! the morning of our marriage approaches.
FIGARO: }

How sweet to my tender spouse is
                your

this pretty, charming little hat that Susanna made herself.

No. 2   Duet

FIGARO: If by night the Countess should want you—
Ding, ding, ding, ding, in two paces you'll be at her side.
Or then, on occasion, if his lordship should want me,
Dong, dong, dong, dong, in three leaps I am there at his side.
SUSANNA: So if one morning the dearest Count should call you, ding, ding, ding, ding,
And send you three miles away,
Ding, ding, dong, dong, to my door the devil will bring him,
And he's here in just three leaps.
FIGARO: Susanna, hush, hush!
SUSANNA: Now listen—
FIGARO: Tell me quickly!
SUSANNA: If you want to hear the rest, discard your suspicions, which do me wrong.

FIGARO: I want to hear the rest.
          My doubts and suspicions make my heart cold!

No. 3   Aria

FIGARO: If you wish to dance, your lordship,
          My guitar will play the tune, yes, play the tune.
          If you wish to come to my school,
          I'll teach you to cut capers, yes, I'll teach you.
          I will know how—but softly,
          The better to discover your secret tricks.
          Hiding cleverness, using cleverness,
          Goading here, jesting there,
          All your intrigue I will overthrow.
          If you wish to dance, your lordship,
          My guitar will play the tune, play the tune!

Wolfgang Amadeus Mozart

(1756–1791)

Symphony No. 40 in G Minor, K. 550

Recognized at the age of four as a child prodigy, Mozart made his first concert tour when he was six and composed his first published pieces before another year had passed. Composing seemingly without effort and performing brilliantly, he became the toast of European capitals and the honored guest of royal houses. He was awarded the Order of the Golden Spur by the Pope and appointed "Chamber Composer" to the Emperor. Despite all this acclaim, in 1788 Mozart found himself poverty-stricken and still seeking the benevolent patron he was never to find. His last three symphonies, of which this is the middle one, were all composed within a period of about six weeks early in the summer of that year.

No more important form was developed by the Classical composers than the form in which the first, second, and fourth movements of this work are cast, the *sonata-allegro*. Sometimes called *sonata form* and sometimes called *first-movement form*, a sonata-allegro consists, typically, of three main sections. In the line score, these sections begin as indicated below:

	first movement measure	second movement measure	fourth movement measure
EXPOSITION	1	1	1
DEVELOPMENT	101	53	125
RECAPITULATION	164	74	206

In the exposition, the themes are stated, connected by transitions. These themes are then "worked out" in the development section—taken apart into fragments that are pitted against each other in counterpoint and presented in various guises while various keys are explored. In the recapitulation, the themes are restated (although in modified form) as a reminder of what material the composer had had to develop.

The third movement, like most regular Classical third movements, is a *minuet and trio* (*menuetto-trio*), a name that recalls the importance of dance music in the origins of instrumental concert music. The minuet contains two tunes, labeled in the line score "a" and "b" and presented in two repeated parts so that we hear them in this order: aababa. The form of the trio is identical, ccdcdc. (The trio was given that name in an earlier time when it was performed by two solo instruments and continuo; here the instrumentation of the orchestra is reduced and the texture is lightened.) At the end of the trio is the notation *Menuetto D.C.;* this indicates a return to the beginning (*da capo,* "to the head") of the minuet, which, performed this time without repeats, rounds out the *ternary* (three-part) form.

The combination of a fast first movement in sonata-allegro form, a slow second movement, a dance-like third movement in three-part form, and a fast finale is customary in Classical symphonies.

"K. 550" appended to the title refers to the listing of this work in the *Köchel Verzeichniss*, an index that lists in chronological order more than six hundred of Mozart's compositions.

Questions for Self-Testing

1. In measures 20–21 of the first movement
   a. the beginning of a new phrase overlaps the end of the old phrase
   b. a new key is established
   c. a new rhythm appears

2. In measures 30–33, two features are
   a. staccato notes
   b. sequences
   c. inversions

3. The development section of the first movement is concerned mostly with
   a. material from Theme I
   b. material from Theme II
   c. material from the transition

4. Some modification of the transition in the exposition is expected in the recapitulation. In this recapitulation, the area between the beginning of the transition and the beginning of Theme II amounts to
   a. a second exposition
   b. a second development section
   c. an extension of Theme I

5. In measures 4–6, 9, and 12–14 of the second movement, persistent repeated notes at the same pitch are heard in what instruments?
   a. flutes
   b. oboes
   c. horns

6. The form of the third movement, a minuet and trio, may be diagrammed
   a. aba   cdc
   b. aababa   ccdcdc
   c. aababa   ccdcdc   aba
   d. aababa   ccdcdc   aababa

7. Which theme is thoroughly worked out in the development section of the finale?

   a. Theme I, first motive
   b. Theme I, second motive
   c. Theme II

8. In the development section of the fourth movement, which theme is almost completely neglected?

   a. Theme I, first motive
   b. Theme I, second motive
   c. Theme II

Wolfgang Amadeus Mozart

Symphony No. 40 in G Minor, K. 550 (1788)

First Movement: Sonata-allegro form

Second Movement: Sonata-allegro form

Exposition: Theme I

Third Movement: Menuetto–trio

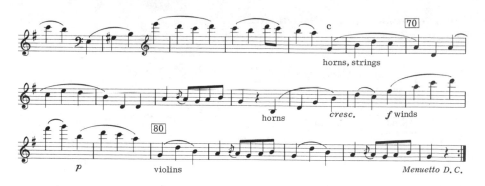

Finale: Sonata-allegro form

Exposition: Theme I, first motive

Allegro assai

Theme I, second motive

violins

Theme II

p

Conclusion (Theme I, second motive)

f violins

Development:

f full orchestra

flute

winds violins

Franz Joseph Haydn

(1732–1809)

Symphony No. 94 in G Major, "Surprise"

Venerated all over Europe in the last decades of the eighteenth century, Haydn had spent most of his life doing what composers did in his time: composing music and supervising its performance in the concerts, operatic productions, and chapel services for the titled aristocrats whose servants they were. His audiences were made up of educated people, and many of his listeners were themselves talented and well-trained amateur musicians. They thoroughly understood the conventions of musical composition and expected the music to appeal to their sense of humor and intellect more than to their emotions.

This slow second movement from one of the symphonies composed for a series of special performances in London in 1791 is one of the classic examples of the theme-and-variations form.

Questions for Self-Testing

1. What could be the reason that this symphony is called "Surprise"?

    a. the occurrence of a loud chord in measure 16
    b. the character of Variation I
    c. the long, sustained chords in Variation II

2. The theme is in a small two-part form that could be diagrammed

    a. ab   ab
    b. ab   ba
    c. aa   bb

3. The third variation features

    a. countermelody
    b. change of key
    c. rhythmic variant

4. Which of these instruments is heard but not mentioned in the line score?

    a. trumpet
    b. trombone
    c. cymbal

5. Which variation is longer than the theme?

    a. Variation I
    b. Variation II
    c. Variation III
    d. Variation IV

Franz Joseph Haydn

Symphony No. 94 in G Major, "Surprise" (1791)

Second Movement: Theme and Variations

Variation IV (Part I)

ff brass, winds

Vigorous counterpoint in violins

110

(Part I, Rhythmic variation)

p vln

120

(Part II)

(Melodic ornamentation)

(Part II, with counterpoint)

130

pp

f full orch.

End of Part II heard with this counterpoint

Coda   140

ff

(Part I, fragment)   (Part I, with new harmony)

p   oboe

150

pp winds, strings

Franz Joseph Haydn

(1732–1809)

String Quartet in G Minor, Op. 74, No. 3

The title *String Quartet in G Minor* is inadequate to identify a quartet by a composer as prolific as Haydn, whose works include three quartets in the key of G minor. "Op. 74, No. 3" gives the remaining information needed to identify this as the third quartet of the set of quartets numbered as Op. 74 (abbreviation for *opus*, "work"), which dates from 1793.

Both the first and fourth movements of this quartet are in sonata-allegro form. The first theme of the first movement is presented as a series of motives.

The second movement is labeled "Ternary form. ABA Coda." A ternary form may be as simple as a plainsong setting of the *Kyrie*, in which one melody is used for *Kyrie eleison*, a contrasting melody is used for *Christe eleison*, and the original melody returns for the final *Kyrie eleison*. Such a simple form would be diagrammed "ABA." The form of this movement is not that simple, however. The A section is in itself a form resembling the minuet, aababa. The B section is brief, featuring upward rather than downward melodic directions. The concluding A section is a small aba form that virtually amounts to a variation on the original material.

Questions for Self-Testing

1. The transition in the exposition of the first movement is built from the rhythm of

   a. Theme I, first motive
   b. Theme I, second motive
   c. Theme I, third motive
   d. new material

2. The beginning of the development section of the first movement sounds like

   a. the beginning of the exposition
   b. Theme II
   c. a fugue

3. Which important musical idea is not recapitulated in the first movement?

   a. Theme I, first motive
   b. Theme I, second motive
   c. Theme I, third motive

4. Compared with its appearance in the exposition, Theme II in the re-capitulation of the first movement is

    a. in a different key
    b. faster
    c. inverted

5. A reason why this quartet is sometimes called "The Rider" might be the

    a. rhythm of Theme I, first motive
    b. contour of Theme II
    c. key of G minor

6. The theme of the trio in the third movement most closely resembles which motive from the first movement?

    a. Theme I, first motive
    b. Theme I, second motive
    c. Theme I, third motive

7. In the finale, a feature of measure 6 is

    a. staccato notes
    b. wide leaps in the melody
    c. notes articulated between beats

8. The feature of measure 6 in the finale named in the question above is developed from measure 63 through measure _____ .

Franz Joseph Haydn

String Quartet in G Minor, Op. 74, No. 3 (1793)

First Movement: Sonata-allegro form

Exposition: Theme I, first motive

Second Movement: Ternary form. ABA coda

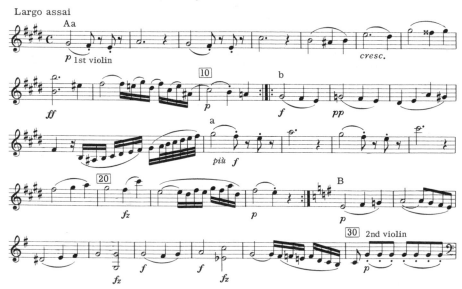

Third Movement: Menuetto-trio

Finale: Sonata-allegro form

Exposition: Theme I, first motive

Allegro con brio   Theme I, second motive

Theme II

Ludwig van Beethoven
(1770–1827)

Piano Sonata in C Minor, Op. 13, "Pathétique"

As the nineteenth century began, Beethoven was in Vienna, active as a composer, as a pianist mainly performing his own works, and as a teacher of piano. Although his earliest works bear some resemblance to those of Haydn and Mozart, his later works are imbued with Romanticism.

As a capitalized word, "Romantic" is usually applied to the music of the nineteenth century, which is characterized by the emotionalism and dramaticism of its style; conceived for virtuoso performers, it is subjectively expressive of a wide gamut of moods and emotions.

The rhythm of Romantic music, an important aspect of its expressiveness, is complicated and flexible, with slowings and quickenings of the pulse, sudden dramatic tempo changes, and unexpected pauses.

The rather heavy texture of most Romantic music features a prominent melody supported by rich, sonorous chords, with considerable dissonance to create emotional tensions. Tonality is an important force in the music, but the methods used in earlier styles to change keys were often so exploited that the overall tonality is blurred. The phrases in Romantic music are usually irregular and the cadences are often bridged over and concealed.

This sonata, completed in the last year of the eighteenth century, adheres in many respects to the dictates of form in the Classical sonata, a work for solo instrument with or without an accompanying keyboard instrument in three movements, fast-slow-fast, the first movement being in sonata-allegro form.

There are also clear signs in this sonata of Romantic tendencies: the dramaticism and moodiness of the slow introduction to the first movement; the number of dynamic markings in the score, coupled with words suggestive of mood such as *con brio* (with brilliance) and *dolce* (sweetly); thick-sounding, low-register chords like the one with which the piece begins; and the virtuosity demanded of the performer.

Both the second and third movements are in *rondo* form, a form in which the main theme makes alternate appearances with contrasting subsidiary themes—for example, ABACA.

Questions for Self-Testing

1. Measure 2 is related to measure 1 by

    a. repetition
    b. sequence
    c. imitation
    d. inversion

2. The basic texture of the work is
    a. two or more prominent melodies heard together
    b. prominent melody with chordal accompaniment
    c. monophonic melody unaccompanied

3. In measures 140–143 is heard a fragment of
    a. the introduction
    b. Theme I
    c. Theme II
    d. the closing theme

4. Theme I is recapitulated exactly, without modification, until measure
   _____ .

5. Theme II is recapitulated
    a. after the closing theme
    b. in a different key
    c. in augmentation
    d. in diminution

6. The first theme of the slow movement is heard twice in the first sixteen
   measures. The second appearance occurs
    a. in the same key but in a higher register
    b. with a thicker accompaniment
    c. in a different key

7. The first theme of the third movement most closely resembles which
   theme of the first movement?
    a. Theme I
    b. Theme II
    c. the closing theme

Ludwig van Beethoven

Piano Sonata No. 8 in C Minor, Op. 13, "Pathétique" (1799)

First Movement: Sonata-allegro form

Introduction

Closing Theme

Second Movement: Rondo. ABACA coda

Third Movement: Rondo. ABACABA coda

Ludwig van Beethoven
(1770–1827)

Symphony No. 5 in C Minor, Op. 67

By 1807, the year in which Beethoven completed this symphony, the Western world had witnessed the dissolution of the Holy Roman Empire, the upheavals of the French and American revolutions, and the beginnings of the Industrial Revolution. Beethoven was himself something of a revolutionary. While his older colleagues had worked as servants in the courts of noblemen, he accepted such commissions as he chose to accept, made business deals with publishers, took in proceeds from concerts, gave piano lessons, and was servant to no man.

Free of the composer's traditional role of servitude, Beethoven began composing music that ignored many of the restraints expected in music for the Establishment at the opening of the nineteenth century. One major change, immediately evident in this symphony, is in the instrumentation of the orchestra. The scoring for the wind instruments requires a larger string choir than was used in the Classical orchestra, and the winds are further augmented in the finale with a piccolo, double bassoon, and three trombones. The strings, which play almost constantly in Classical symphonies, are silent from time to time as the wind instruments are given more responsible roles.

The symphony also reflects many innovations in form. In the first movement, the recapitulation is extended to a length greater than that of the exposition and development sections combined. The slow movement, instead of being a Classical theme and variations, is a free set of variations on two themes. In place of the traditional minuet, the third movement is a gruffly good-humored piece in the nature of a *scherzo* (joke). It proceeds *attacca* (without pause) into the finale, which contains thematic material from the third movement. Tempos change within movements, and the entire work is saturated with the four-note motive with which it begins.

Questions for Self-Testing

1. By the time we get to measure 21 we have heard how many of these devices?
    a. repetition
    b. sequence
    c. imitation
    d. imitation by inversion

2. While Theme II is being stated, the cello and bass sections offer five statements of
    a. a preview of the closing theme
    b. a rapid ascending scale
    c. the rhythm of the four-note motive

3. At the beginning of the development section we hear
   a. a fragment of Theme II
   b. an augmentation of the closing theme
   c. the four-note motive in a new key

4. Through measure 178 the development section is concerned with
   a. Theme I
   b. Theme II
   c. the closing theme

5. In measures 196–227, the development section is concerned with
   a. the rhythm of the four-note motive
   b. notes 4–5 of Theme II
   c. the closing theme
   d. new material

6. Between measures 409 and 415, the winds offer
   a. the four-note motive
   b. notes 4–5 of Theme II in diminution
   c. an inversion of the closing theme
   d. new material

7. Conspicuously silent in measures 133–142 of the second movement are the
   a. flutes
   b. oboes
   c. clarinets
   d. strings

8. Which two elements are featured in measures 191–194?
   a. the rhythm of the motive
   b. ascending scales in imitation
   c. a fragment of the second theme
   d. a descending scale in the brasses

9. Measures 219–222 feature
   a. woodwinds
   b. brasses
   c. timpani
   d. strings

10. The theme beginning at measure 19 in the third movement resembles
    a. the contour of Theme I, first movement
    b. the rhythm of Theme I, first movement
    c. the contour of Theme I, second movement
    d. the rhythm of Theme I, second movement

11. Measures 236–237 of the third movement are related to the beginning
of the movement by a partial

    a. inversion

    b. sequence

    c. augmentation

    d. diminution

Ludwig van Beethoven

Symphony No. 5 in C Minor (1807)

First Movement: Sonata-allegro form

Second Movement: Free variations on two themes

Theme I
Andante con moto

Third Movement: Scherzo with trio

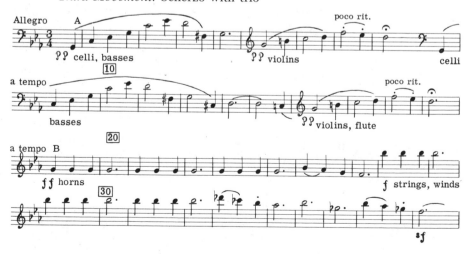

(Theme I, A; canonic imitation in basses)

strings *f* winds   *ff* full orch.

Franz Schubert
(1797–1828)

Der Erlkönig

Much of the music composed in the nineteenth century was intended to be performed in the intimacy of a salon rather than in a large concert hall. The *art song*, called *chanson* in French and *Lied* in German (plural *Lieder*), is a setting of a poetic text for solo singer with piano accompaniment.

This is one of the more than six hundred *Lieder* composed by Schubert during his short life. In 1815, the year *Der Erlkönig* was composed, the eighteen-year-old Schubert produced more than one hundred and thirty songs, two symphonies, a dozen or more works for chorus, a string quartet, several piano pieces, and five operas, all while making a meager living as a school teacher.

Striving for a perfect matching of poetic text and music, the composer of *Lieder* uses musical devices to reflect meanings in the text. Some of the more obvious examples of text-painting in *Der Erlkönig* are the fast tempo that reflects a sense of haste; the rapid repeated notes in the accompaniment that sound like galloping hoofbeats; the harp-like figure that accompanies the Erl King's seductive "Willst, feiner Knabe, du mit mir geh'n? meine Töchter sollen dich warten schön"; and the pair of abrupt chords that terminate the song, suggesting the finality of death.

Questions for Self-Testing

1. Each time the father speaks to the child, his uneasiness is text-painted by
    a. an agitated figure in the extreme low range
    b. cessation of rhythmic activity in the bass
    c. cessation of the "galloping" figure

2. Each time the father identifies the things that the child imagines to be the Erl King or his daughters, his reassurances end with
    a. a rising melodic line
    b. a strong cadence in the accompaniment
    c. increasing rhythmic activity in the accompaniment

3. The child speaks to the father four times. His increasing consternation is reflected by the fact that each recurrence is
    a. higher than before
    b. faster than before

Franz Schubert

Der Erlkönig (1815)

(Text by Johann Wolfgang von Goethe. English translation on p. 117.)

Schnell (Allegro)

Wer rei - tet so spät durch Nacht und Wind? Es ist der Va - ter mit sei - nem Kind; er hat den Kna - ben wohl in dem Arm, er fasst ihn si - cher, er hält ihn warm. Mein Sohn, was birgst du so bang dein Ge - sicht? Siehst, Va - ter, du den Erl - kö - nig nicht? den

Er - len - kö - nig mit Kron' und Schweif? Mein Sohn, es ist ein

Ne - bel - streif. "Du lie - bes Kind, komm', geh' mit

mir! gar schö - ne Spie - le spiel' ich mit dir; manch' bun - te

Blu - men sind an dem Strand; mei - ne Mut - ter hat manch' gül - den Ge-

-wand." Mein Va - ter, mein Va - ter, und hö - rest du nicht, was

Erl - len - kö - nig mir lei - se ver -spricht? Sei ru - hig, blei - be

ru - hig, mein Kind; in dür - ren Blät - tern säu - selt der Wind.

"Willst, fei - ner Kna - be, du mit mir geh'n? mei-ne Töch-ter sol - len dich

war - ten schön; mei-ne Töch - ter füh - ren den nächt - li -chen Reih'n und

wie - gen und tan - zen und sin - gen dich ein, sie wie-gen und tan-zen und

sin - gen dich ein." Mein Va - ter, mein Va - ter, und siehst du nicht

dort Erl - kö - nigs Töch - ter am dü - stern Ort? Mein Sohn, mein

Sohn, ich seh' es ge - nau, es schei - nen die al - ten Wei - den so grau.

piano

"Ich lie - be dich, mich

reizt dei - ne schö - ne Ge - stalt, und bist du nicht wil - lig, so brauch' ich Ge-

-walt.'' Mein Va - ter, mein Va - ter, jetzt fasst er mich an! Erl - kö - nig

hat mir ein Leid's ge - tan! Dem Va - ter grau - set's, er

rei - tet ge - schwind, er hält in Ar - men das äch - zen - de Kind,

er - reicht den Hof mit Müh und Not;

Recit.   piano

in sei-nen Ar - men das Kind war tot.

The Erl King

Who gallops so late through night and wind?
It is the father with his child.
He has the boy so safe in his arm;
He clasps him tightly, he keeps him warm.

My son, why do you hide your face in terror?
Do you see, Father, that the Erl King is near?
The Erl King with crown and robe?
My son, it is a cloud of mist.

"My lovely child, come, go with me!
Such pleasant games I'll play with you.
So many flowers bloom there on the shore,
And my mother has many golden robes for you!"

My father, my father, now truly you hear
What the Erl King whispers so softly to me?
Be quiet, please be quiet, my child;
It is but the dead leaves stirred by the wind. .

"Will you, my lovely boy, go with me?
My fair daughters will wait on you.
My fair daughters dance in the revels all night.
They'll sing and they'll dance and they'll rock you to sleep;
They'll sing and they'll dance and they'll rock you to sleep!"

My father, my father, and do you not see
The Erl King's daughters in that dark spot?
My son, my son, I see well enough,
It is only the old willows so gray!

"I love you, child, your beautiful form inflames me!
And if you're not willing, I must then use force!"
My father, my father, he now grasps my arm,
The Erl King has seized me, his grasp hurts me!"

The father shudders; he rides like the wind,
The sick, dying child held in his arms.
He reaches home with fear and dread;
In his arms, the child was dead.

Frederic Chopin
(1810–1849)

Etude in E Major, Op. 10, No. 3

Among the most romantic of musical personages in the nineteenth century were the composer-pianists, of whom the Polish-born Chopin was one. They dazzled audiences with virtuoso performances, especially of their own compositions.

Composed while Chopin was establishing himself as composer, pianist, and teacher of piano in Paris early in the 1830's, this etude is the third of the twelve that make up Opus 10. Each etude is a study of some particular technical problem in pianistic performance (the E major etude is concerned with double-note fingering problems in the pianist's right hand), but Chopin's *Etudes* are more than merely practice pieces and are still frequently performed in piano recitals.

The melody of the first part of this etude invites the pianist to make his instrument "sing" the line, and the accompaniment, through its repeated notes, permits the many gradual increases and decreases in volume that are called for in the score. In addition to dynamics, the score is full of directions for the performer to alter tempo and to establish mood, such as *con fuoco* (with fire), *con bravura* (with boldness), and *smorzando* (dying away).

Questions for Self-Testing

1. Virtuoso display passages make up the
   a. first part
   b. first half of the second part
   c. second half of the second part

2. In your recording of this piece, there is a decided tendency toward
   a. steady tempo
   b. unsteady tempo

3. The material of the first part returns in measure 62. How many measures are repeated intact? _____

Frederic Chopin
Etude in E Major, Op. 10, No. 3 (c. 1830)

Ternary form: ABA

Richard Wagner

(1813–1883)

Tristan and Isolde

The powerful movement in the nineteenth century toward the alliance of music with the other arts reached a culmination in the *music dramas* of Richard Wagner, in which literary, theatrical, and musical elements assume equal importance. In earlier operas, and in many later ones as well, the dramatic situation is often hardly more than an excuse for the existence of the music. Wagner considered the theatrical text, or *libretto*, to be equally important, and in contrast to general practice he wrote his own librettos, many of them based on Teutonic legends.

Wagner composed *Tristan and Isolde* between 1857 and 1859, a time of great personal stress, when he was living as a political exile in Switzerland and Italy, engaged in unsatisfactory business dealings with publishers, harassed by creditors, and involved in an extra-marital affair and plagued by the resulting friction with his wife. The work is a tragedy of love and death. Tristan, a knight in the service of his uncle, the king of Cornwall, and Isolde, a princess of Ireland who is to become the king's bride, unknowingly drink a powerful love potion. They find themselves helplessly, hopelessly, and passionately in love. Their sensuous love duet in Act II is interrupted at its climactic moment when they are discovered by the king. Tristan is wounded in the ensuing fight. In the final scene of the drama, Tristan dies of his wound, and the tragedy is concluded by Isolde's *Liebestod* ("Love Death"), at the end of which she falls, "transfigured," on the body of her lover. Much of the music of the *Liebestod* is drawn from the love duet, but it does not attain there the searing and rapturous climax reached (at measure 61) in the *Liebestod*.

The large orchestra called for in Wagner's music dramas is not merely an accompaniment for the singer; it is important in the narration as well. By means of a device called the *leitmotif*, a musical idea representing a person, place, thing, or concept of special significance, Wagner used the orchestra to comment upon the action, reminisce about past events, and convey insight into psychological aspects of the drama.

Wagner did not himself assign names to his motives. Later writers have listed and named them; as efforts to second-guess the composer, they may or may not have some connection with his thinking. An understanding of what some of the motives may have been intended to represent will be helpful in gaining access to the music.

In the first pair of measures, Isolde sings two motives that, sequenced and imitated, are the thematic basis for the next seventeen measures. The first motive is the principal motive of the entire *Liebestod*. The second has been called "The Pains of Death." At measure 19 the clarinet introduces a motive that has been called "Ecstasy." In measures 25–26 the violins introduce motives that have been identified with "Tristan" and "Desire." In measure 43 the violins introduce the motive called "Rapture."

While some access to the music may be gained through motives with names, however questionable the names may be, careful listening to the harmony brings some special insights. During the first twelve measures, the tonalities change almost constantly. Further changing of tonalities occurs as the music continues until, a few measures before the monumental climax in measure 60, the music settles into a stable tonality as suspense and anticipation swell and grow. The harmonic tension is maintained after the climax by dissonance that bridges each anticipated cadence until relaxation is finally felt three measures before the end of the piece.

Questions for Self-Testing

1. The instrument heard for the first time in measure 9 is

    a. trumpet
    b. double bass
    c. harp

2. The motive introduced in measure 19 is sung by Isolde in measure 34 in

    a. inversion
    b. augmentation
    c. diminution

3. The orchestral parts in measures 19–25 feature the motive of measure 19 and the motive of measure

    a. 1
    b. 2
    c. 1 inverted
    d. 2 inverted

4. In measures 33–38 the high woodwinds play

    a. a fragment of the motive of measure 19
    b. the motive from measure 1
    c. the motive from measure 2

5. In measures 39–41 the bassoon and English horn play the motive from measure

    a. 19
    b. 25
    c. 26

6. In measures 61–64 the brass instruments play

    a. rapid fanfare patterns
    b. rapid scale passages
    c. sustained chords

Richard Wagner

Tristan and Isolde (1859)

Liebestod

"Love Death"

How soft and quiet his smile as his eyes open. See, friends, do you not see how, clothed and transfigured in starlight, he gleams ever brighter? Do you not see how his courageous heart swells and throbs, full and majestic in his bosom? How his sweet breath escapes ecstatically, softly through his lips? Look! Do you not feel and see?

Do I alone hear this melody—wondrous and delicate sounds lamenting ecstasy, telling all, serenely ringing about me, penetrating, soothing, boiling up and more brightly echoing about me? Are these billows gentle zephyrs? Are they clouds of rapturous fragrance as they swell and roar about me? Shall I breathe? Shall I listen? Shall I drink? Shall I plunge in? Breathe my last in sweet fragrances? To sink in the billowing, resounding sounds, unconscious, in the swirling breath of the world—greatest ecstasy!

Giuseppe Verdi
(1813–1901)

Aïda

Dear to the Italian heart is *bel canto* (beautiful singing) on the operatic stage.

Verdi, the dominant figure in Italian opera in his time, was venerated by his countrymen for his music and for his patriotism. The name of Verdi became an acrostic cheer for the king: Victor Emmanuel **Re** d'Italia.

Aïda, first performed in Cairo in 1871 to celebrate the completion of the Suez Canal, has an Egyptian setting. As in most Italian opera, the solo voice dominates everything in lovely, soaring melodies with high notes which invite lingering attention. The first part of the scene given here functions like a recitative, establishing the dramatic situation for the solos and duet of the doomed lovers.

For this last scene of the opera the stage is in two levels: above, the golden temple of Vulcan; below, the vault in which Egyptian General Radames is to be buried alive, falsely convicted of treason as a result of his love for the captive Ethiopian Princess Aïda. Radames finds Aïda hiding in the vault, to die with him. Those in the temple above invoke the god Fthà as the lovers say goodbye and die in each other's arms. Amneris, the Egyptian princess in love with Radames, prays to Isis for his soul.

Questions for Self-Testing

1. In measures 6–7 the voice of Radames is

    a. accompanied by strings
    b. accompanied by woodwinds
    c. unaccompanied

2. In measures 36–42, the orchestra plays

    a. two throbbing chords per measure
    b. a sustained chord
    c. nothing

3. In measures 46–56, the orchestra plays

    a. scale passages
    b. guitar-like chords
    c. nothing

4. In measures 79–87 the prominent instrument is

    a. oboe
    b. trombone
    c. harp

Giuseppe Verdi

Aïda (1871)

Act IV, Scene II

(English translation on pp. 134–35.)

RADAMES: The fatal stone is now closing upon me.
    Here is my tomb.
    Nevermore shall I behold the light of day.
    I shall never see Aïda again!
    Aïda, where are you now?
    May you at least live happily
    And may my awful doom never reach your ear!
    What a groan was that!
    It is a phantom . . . a vision . . .
    No! the form is human . . .
    Heaven! Aïda!
AÏDA: It is I.
RADAMES: You in this tomb!
AÏDA: My heart foresaw your frightful sentence.
    Into this tomb that opened for you
    I crept unseen,
    And here, far away from every human glance,
    In your arms I desire to die.
RADAMES: To die! So pure and lovely!
    To die, for love of me,
    From your years of flowering to flee life!
    You whom heaven created for love alone,
    And I destory you for having loved you!
    No, I will not die!
    I loved you too much! you are too lovely!

AÏDA: Do you see? the radiant angel of death
           Draws near to lead us to eternal joys above
           On his wings of gold.
           Now I see heaven reveal itself;
           There every grief ceases,
           There begin the ecstasies of immortal love.

CHORUS: Almighty Fthà, animating spirit of the world,
           Ah! Ah! We invoke thee, we invoke thee!

AÏDA: Sorrowful chant!

RADAMES: It is the exultation of the priests.

AÏDA: It is our hymn of death.

RADAMES: (trying to move the stone) Nor can my strong arms remove this fatal stone!

AÏDA: In vain! Everything for us on earth is finished.

RADAMES: It is true! It is true!

AÏDA: O earth, farewell, farewell valley of sorrows,
           Dream of joy that vanishes in grief.
           To us heaven opens,
           Heaven opens and the fleeing souls
           Fly to the light of eternal day.

RADAMES: O earth, farewell, (etc.)

CHORUS: Almighty Fthà, we invoke thee, (etc.)

AÏDA AND
RADAMES: Ah! heaven reveals itself.
           O earth, farewell, (etc.)

AMNERIS: Peace, I implore, adored Radames.
           May Isis be appeased, may Isis open heaven to you!
           Peace, I implore, peace, peace!

Peter Ilich Tchaikovsky
(1840–1893)

Romeo and Juliet

Having abandoned an occupation as a law clerk during his early twenties for a career in music, Tchaikovsky spent the next twenty years in an almost overwhelming struggle. He overworked himself in teaching and composing, his early compositions were poorly received, and his life was complicated by a brief but disastrous marriage. Shortly before 1880, suffering from depression and on the verge of nervous collapse, Tchaikovsky finally found a patroness whose generosity gave him financial security, and the recognition he had so long sought for his works began to come about. In that year, he revised and reworked, for the second time, his *Romeo and Juliet*.

This is a highly emotional work, with powerfully contrasting moods of serenity, dejection, and triumph and moments of tender eroticism. As is usual in Tchaikovsky's orchestral music, the melodies, whether melting or bold, are prominently presented, often by wind instruments.

Questions for Self-Testing

1. The combination of instruments that present the Friar's theme might have been chosen to imitate the sound of what instrument? _____

2. The purpose of measures 10–37 and 52–76 is to
   a. state themes
   b. increase intensity
   c. establish a mood

3. Abrupt, crashing chords, possibly representing swordplay, are presented by wind and percussion instruments in measures _____ .

4. A transition begins in measure 163, made from a
   a. three-note rising figure
   b. three-note falling figure
   c. four-note rhythmic pattern

5. The nature of Juliet's theme might be interpreted as a reflection of her
   a. languorous beauty
   b. ladylike poise
   c. immaturity

6. The prominent motive sequenced in the solo horn under the statement of Romeo's theme in measures 212–228 is
   a. new material
   b. a fragment of the Friar's theme
   c. a fragment of Juliet's theme

Peter Ilich Tchaikovsky

Romeo and Juliet (1880)

Modified sonata-allegro form

Strife theme developed

Johannes Brahms

(1833–1897)

Piano Concerto No. 2 in B Flat Major, Op. 83

Brahms' musical career included playing piano as a tavern entertainer, traveling as a concert pianist with one of the best concert violinists of his time, and conducting the *Singakademie* and the *Gesellschaft der Musikfreunde* (Society of Friends of Music) in Vienna, before he awoke to fame as his works began to be performed by prestigious artists.

With a modesty and caution not typical among creative artists, Brahms invited eminent composers to criticize his compositions as he completed them. He waited until his forty-third year before venturing to compose his first symphony and, severely critical of his own work, he destroyed the manuscripts of all his music that he felt was second rate.

Evolving from the *concerto grosso*, the Classical concerto became a work for instrumental solo with orchestra, in three movements—fast-slow-fast. The first movement is a sonata-allegro form, which is often modified by a double exposition, one by the orchestra and one by the soloist. Brahms' concerto is not typical of the concertos composed during the 1880's, in which the soloist was given ample opportunity for flamboyant displays of virtuosity. At a time when most composers were preoccupied with the seemingly endless orchestral color possibilities afforded by combinations of winds and percussion instruments, Brahms continued to develop traditions inherited from his Classical predecessors; he scored this concerto for the wind instruments commonly used a hundred years earlier.

Matters of form in the *Concerto No. 2* reveal clearly that Brahms' reverence for Classical procedures and forms did not stifle his originality. Instead of the usual three movements, there are four. And the form of the fourth movement is one for which there is no name. The opening thematic material is stated in measures 1–59. After a brief transition, contrasting material is stated and developed in measures 65–164. The opening material returns and is developed in measures 165–308. The contrasting material returns and is developed in measures 308–395, and the *coda* concludes the piece.

Questions for Self-Testing

1. The instruments heard at the beginning are piano and
   a. flutes
   b. horns
   c. violas
   d. timpani

2. In measures 31–34 the material is

    a. new
    b. transitional

3. In measures 65–80 the piano is

    a. accompanying the orchestra
    b. accompanied by the orchestra
    c. silent

4. In measures 149–164 the material is

    a. new
    b. transitional

5. Accompanying the oboe solo in measures 165–172 are piano and

    a. strings
    b. woodwinds
    c. brasses

6. In measures 212–228 the orchestra is

    a. reduced to a few strings
    b. sustaining a chord
    c. silent

7. The material at the beginning of the *coda* is

    a. made from the opening material
    b. made from the contrasting material
    c. new material

Johannes Brahms

Piano Concerto No. 2 in B Flat Major, Op. 83 (1881)

Fourth Movement

Charles Ives

(1874–1954)

Variations on "America" (1891)

The son of a bandmaster in Danbury, Connecticut, Ives absorbed during his childhood the sounds and combinations of sounds that he heard around him. He might have heard and remembered, for instance, a hymn being sung in church in one key while the village band played something in another key. In incorporating such effects in his music, Ives discovered some devices and techniques that were to become common in twentieth-century music.

In this set of variations written for the organ, for example, measures 13–14 are unexpectedly, unexplainedly, and incongruously dissonant. In the first interlude, the right hand plays in one key and is quarreled with by the left hand in imitation but in another, seemingly hostile, key.

Ives' note to the performer "Ad lib. till°" (at pleasure till°) may be understood to mean that the performer is to choose his own tempo or is to improvise or is to omit the passage if he chooses. Such indeterminate directions, almost unknown in nineteenth-century composition, have become important in *aleatory* (or "chance") music in this century.

Ives' innovations are the more remarkable when we realize that he composed as a hobby (he was in the insurance business) and in comparative isolation. At the time he wrote this piece, he was still in his teens and had been exposed to the music of no later composer than Debussy. He has justly been called the most original American composer.

Questions for Self-Testing

1. Variation I is made by

    a. alteration of rhythm of theme
    b. striking rhythmic accompaniment
    c. added countermelody

2. Variation II is made by

    a. alteration of rhythm of theme
    b. striking rhythmic accompaniment
    c. added countermelody

3. Variation III is made by

    a. alteration of rhythm of theme
    b. striking rhythmic accompaniment
    c. added countermelody

4. Variation IV is made by

    a. alteration of rhythm of theme

    b. striking rhythmic accompaniment

    c. added countermelody

5. In measures 79–81 the theme is treated in

    a. augmentation

    b. diminution

    c. inversion

Charles Ives

Variations on "America" (1891)

Antonin Dvořák

(1841–1904)

Symphony No. 9 in E Minor, "From the New World"

Composed during Dvořák's three-year tenure as director of the National Conservatory of Music in New York City, the symphony "From the New World" was first performed by the New York Philharmonic Orchestra in 1893, by which time Dvořák was famous as a composer and conductor throughout the Western world. At one time called *Symphony No. 5*, it is now known as No. 9.

Dvořák's interest in the folk music of his native Bohemia was paralleled during his residence in the United States by an interest in American folk music, and many of the themes in this symphony display some of the characteristics of the music of American Indians and blacks. Compare, for instance, the rise and the fall of Theme III of the first movement with the rise and fall of the tune "Swing Low, Sweet Chariot." The theme of the largo is so song-like that words have been fitted to it to make a song called "Goin' Home."

In some ways, this work is Classical in its symphonic form: the first of the four movements is a sonata-allegro with a slow introduction; the tempo of the second movement is slow; the third movement is a scherzo with trio; and the fourth movement is a fast and triumphant finale. In other ways, however, there are departures from the Classical symphonic tradition: there are changes of tempo within movements; some of the themes are so closely related that they seem to be different versions of the same thing; themes from earlier movements are quoted in later movements; the aababa form of the Classical scherzo is truncated to aaba; and the entire work is imbued with the emotionalism common to nineteenth-century music.

Questions for Self-Testing

1. In measures 16 and 18, Theme I is "previewed" in
   a. rhythm
   b. shape
   c. tempo

2. In what measures is Theme II "previewed"?
   a. 53 and 65
   b. 69 and 71
   c. 74 and 76

3. The first four notes of Theme III and the first four notes of Theme I are identical in
   a. rhythm
   b. shape
   c. tempo

4. Measures 300–303 are made from a fragment of Theme I

    a. in augmentation
    b. in diminution
    c. inverted

5. Measures 404–407 and 428–433 are made from fragments of Theme I

    a. in augmentation
    b. in diminution
    c. inverted

6. Variants of the introductory measures of the second movement are heard, later, in measures

    a. 7–10 and 46–49
    b. 54–57 and 78–81
    c. 22–25 and 120–123

7. In the second movement, measure 9 is related to measure 7 by

    a. repetition
    b. sequence
    c. inversion

8. Measures 20–21 are related to measure 19 by

    a. augmentation
    b. diminution
    c. inversion

9. In the third movement, the prominent percussion instruments are timpani and

    a. cymbal
    b. triangle
    c. tom-tom

10. In the fourth movement, the theme that is ignored in the development section is Theme

    a. I
    b. II
    c. III (closing theme)

Antonin Dvořák

Symphony No. 9 in E Minor, "From the New World" (1893)

First Movement: Sonata-allegro form

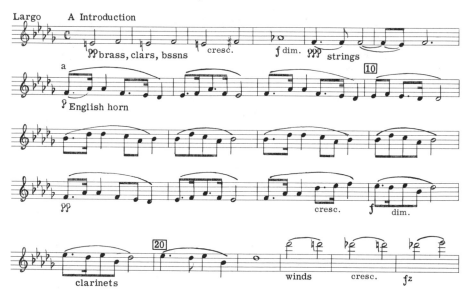

Second Movement: Ternary form

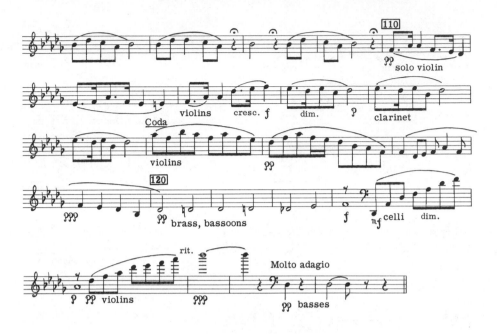

Third Movement: Scherzo with trio

Fourth Movement: Sonata-allegro form

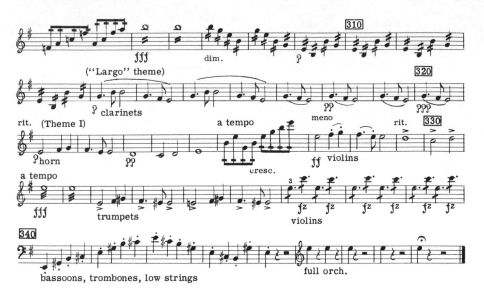

Claude Debussy

(1862–1918)

Prelude to the Afternoon of a Faun

In a reaction against Teutonic formalism and realism, which had dominated European orchestral music in the nineteenth century, Debussy founded a style in France that came to be called Impressionism. Given the name because in some ways the musical style seemed analogous to that of the Impressionist painters, who were preoccupied with colors and the effects of shifting light, Impressionism in music gives paramount importance to effects of tone color.

In this orchestral piece, a hazy, luminous shimmer is created by muted strings and brasses, delicately handled percussion instruments, and solo woodwinds. Instead of vivid blocks of sound from massed brasses, woodwinds, or string choir, we hear individual tone colors highlighted and blended.

At several places in the piece, the effect is that "the light has shifted" on the sound. One of these is in measure 14, where the sound of the solo flute gradually mixes with the sound of the oboe and then disappears as the oboe continues the solo line. Another is heard as the sound of the solo clarinet in measure 20 fades in favor of the color of the solo flute entering in measure 21.

The rhythm, indefinite and subtle, is not conducive to foot-tapping. Sixteen changes of meter signature obscure the metrical structure before measure 55.

The melodies are made of brief fragments sequenced, repeated, and passed from one instrumental color to another. Scales other than the familiar major and minor are used, as in measures 35–36, which are built from a scale using alternate notes on the piano keyboard, called a *whole-tone scale*.

First performed in 1894, the work was inspired by an eclogue of the poet Stephane Mallarmé.

Questions for Self-Testing

1. The stringed instrument prominent in measures 4 and 7 is
    a. viola
    b. cello
    c. harp

2. The violins, heard in prominence for the first time in measure 40, play material from measure
    a. 1
    b. 6
    c. 39

3. The general texture of the piece is

    a. prominent soprano melody supported by chords
    b. equally important simultaneous melodies
    c. lacy and veiled

4. The faun's afternoon is depicted

    a. realistically, with birdsongs and animal noises
    b. in a stylized way, with musical ideas possessing extra-musical significance
    c. symbolically, with allusions and suggestions to stimulate the listener's imagination

Claude Debussy

Prelude to the Afternoon of a Faun (1894)

Ternary form: ABA

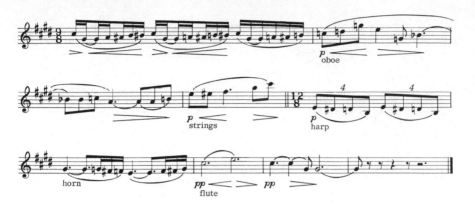

Igor Stravinsky
(1882–1971)

"Sacrificial Dance" from *The Rite of Spring*

Modern music is sometimes said to have begun on May 29, 1913, with the first performance, in Paris, of *The Rite of Spring*. The responses of the audience ranged from feverishly excited acceptance of the work to such outrage and hostility that riotous misconduct kept much of the music from being heard. Not only did the music seem to break most ties with past harmonic, melodic, and rhythmic norms, but the scenery and costumes were anything but pretty, and the choreography was far from that of classical ballet.

Subtitled *Pictures from Pagan Russia*, the ballet concludes with the "Sacrificial Dance (The Chosen One)" and requires an unusually large orchestra: three flutes, a piccolo, and an alto flute; three clarinets, a small E flat clarinet, and an alto clarinet; four bassoons and a contrabassoon; eight horns; four trumpets and a small "Baroque trumpet"; three trombones; two tubas; a large percussion section including two timpanists using a minimum of five kettledrums; and a very large choir of strings.

The elemental force at work in the "Sacrificial Dance" is rhythm, a rhythm that is driving, compelling, exhausting, and extremely complicated. Within the 168 measures of the piece, even in the "simplified" score provided by the composer more than thirty years after the first performance, there are 157 changes of meter. Although the listener is keenly aware of the frenetic rhythmic activity, attempts to participate in the rhythm by bodily movement are continually defeated as the accents of the meter shift.

Because of these constantly changing meters, a line score would be extremely difficult to follow and has therefore not been provided here. The form of the work, however, is a rondo that the listener should have no trouble following without the aid of a line score.

Questions for Self-Testing

1. Throughout the piece, the strings are used primarily
    a. melodically
    b. on sustaining chords
    c. percussively

2. In this work in rondo form, the A section is heard
    a. three times
    b. four times
    c. five times

3. The chords in the first A section seem to be

    a. traditional chords used in untraditional ways

    b. dissonant clusters of tones

4. In the beginning of the B section the harmony

    a. alternates between two chords

    b. is static and unchanging

5. The beginning of the second A section is

    a. exactly like the first

    b. like the first at a different pitch level

    c. like the first with rhythm altered

6. Compared with the first A section, the last A section features chords that are

    a. more dissonant

    b. less dissonant

    c. equally dissonant

Igor Stravinsky
(1882–1971)

Octet for Wind Instruments

Not long after *The Rite of Spring* brought international fame to Stravinsky, he abandoned composing for the large orchestra and turned his attention to less spectacular and more concise forms of musical expression. Like many other composers early in the 1920's, he began to use devices reminiscent of eighteenth-century music, avoiding most of what were thought of as excesses of expanded form, emotionalism, huge orchestras, and grand gestures that were the legacy of the nineteenth century.

Stravinsky's *Octet*, for flute, clarinet, and pairs of bassoons, trumpets, and trombones is one of the works that has been called neoclassic. The score was first published in 1924 and was revised by the composer in 1952.

The form of the second movement is clearly announced in its title, "Theme with Variations." The finale cadence is not conclusive because the last few measures of the movement serve as a transition into the finale, and the last bassoon notes of the movement are the initial notes of the finale.

Questions for Self-Testing

1. The theme is heard

    a. accompanied by staccato chords
    b. accompanied by sustained chords
    c. unaccompanied

2. In its second appearance, the theme is

    a. shortened
    b. lengthened
    c. repeated exactly

3. Variation B has the character of a

    a. lullaby
    b. march
    c. fugue

4. In Variation C the bulk of the accompaniment is

    a. like the "oom-pah-pah" of a waltz
    b. sustained organ-like chords
    c. provided by countermelodies

5. Variation E has the character of a
    a. lullaby
    b. march
    c. fugue

6. The return of Variation A (called by the composer the "ribbons of scales" variation) as an introduction to each of the other variations superimposes upon this theme-and-variations form a suggestion of
    a. basso ostinato
    b. rondo principles
    c. extra-musical connotations

Igor Stravinsky

Octet for Wind Instruments (1924)

Second Movement: Theme and Variations

proceeds without pause
into the finale

Anton Webern

(1883–1945)

Quartet for Violin, Clarinet, Tenor Saxophone, and Piano, Op. 22

Webern's style, which has been called "orchestrated silence," grew out of the work of Arnold Schoenberg (1874–1951), who devised a method of composing in twelve tones related only to each other instead of to a tonal center. Schoenberg and other composers in the first and second decades of the twentieth century thus found themselves composing music that had no tonal center. It became necessary to find something with which to replace the powerful unifying force of tonality, which had been the most important organizing factor in Western music for three centuries. Years of trial-and-error search for a replacement resulted in serial treatment of pitches, composition with rows or sets of the twelve tones of the chromatic scale, the notes represented by all the black and white keys in one octave on the piano.

In the score, trace the notes numbered 0–11 beginning in the saxophone. These twelve tones (none of which is repeated) constitute the "PO," or prime order of the set at its initial pitch. Find and trace the set begun in the right hand of the piano in measure 6. This is P6, the prime form of the set sounding six notes higher than the initial pitch of PO. In addition to the P, or prime, form of the set at twelve different pitch levels, the composer has available also inverted (I) order, retrograde (R) or 11–0 order, and retrograde-inversion (RI) order, each at twelve different pitch levels.

The introduction to this movement consists of a statement of PO imitated (by inversion) by I 10, the inverted form of the set begun ten notes above the initial pitch of PO. The repeated note played by the clarinet in measure 4 functions as the eighth tone of each of the two sets.

The repeated note also signals that its pitch is to become the most important pitch in the piece, and it does. It is equidistant from the highest and lowest notes in the piece (see violin and piano in measure 22) and is sounded twenty-five times, more often than any other note.

The left and right hands in the piano score are treated as two separate instrumental parts, imitating each other (by inversion) throughout the movement. Each hand plays one hundred and forty notes of equal duration (disregarding tempo changes) and is silent for more than twice that number of equivalent rests.

The work is scored for an unusual instrumental combination. At virtually every entrance of each instrument the composer has markings for dynamic level and mode of attack. In this kind of music each note is important because there are so few of them and because of the great care with which each is treated.

The form of this movement bears some resemblance to the Classical sonata-allegro form, with a five-measure introduction, an exposition (measures 6–15) that is repeated, and a development section (measures 16–27) and recapitulation (measures 28–37) that are repeated and followed by a coda.

The first movement of the quartet is of brief duration, being only 2 minutes and 35 seconds long. This brevity is characteristic; Webern's entire lifetime of composing resulted in a corpus of works that have been recorded on four LP records.

Questions for Self-Testing

1. The effect in measures 5, 15, 21, 24, and 37 (a and b) is
   a. transitional
   b. cadential
   c. continuational

2. The first note played by the violin is played, in that register, only by the violin and
   a. clarinet
   b. saxophone
   c. piano

3. The bottom note in the piano (left hand) in measure 14 is played by piano and
   a. saxophone
   b. no other instrument

Quartet for Violin, Clarinet, Tenor Saxophone, and Piano, Op. 22 (1938)

First Movement

Béla Bartók

(1881–1945)

Concerto for Orchestra

Bartók came to the United States in 1940 as a political refugee. He had been recognized in his native Hungary as a pianist, teacher of piano, and expert researcher of folk songs but not as a composer, except of some stage works that had been condemned as immoral or politically unacceptable to the occupying Nazi government. In 1943, unable to hold a position because of illness and living nearly in poverty, Bartók composed this *Concerto for Orchestra;* it has assumed a prominent place in the repertory of American symphony orchestras.

In a Classical concerto, a soloist is featured with the orchestra. In a concerto grosso, a group of instruments is given special prominence. In Bartók's concerto, each instrument or section of instruments of the orchestra is called into soloistic prominence.

Within the first eleven measures of the music we hear indications that the musical materials are being used in twentieth-century ways. For instance, the relationship of the first pair of pitches is called a fourth. For centuries, a fourth in a melodic line had been common (as in the first pitches of "Here Comes the Bride," "O Christmas Tree," and "Taps,") but Bartók uses two of them in a row, a stylistic device characteristic of this century. The importance of melodic fourths in the piece is emphasized in measures 22–29, there being eleven fourths between pairs of adjacent pitches. Another indication of the period style of the piece comes when the flutes begin on a pitch dissonant with that of the bass and then separate into a pair of pitches dissonant with each other.

Questions for Self-Testing

1. Measures 35–38 are made from

    a. Motive A
    b. material in measures 6–11
    c. new material

2. In measure 51 begins a variant of

    a. Motive A
    b. material in measures 6–11
    c. Motive B

3. As Theme IA is presented by the violins, it is

    a. unaccompanied
    b. accompanied by a prominent countermelody
    c. accompanied by short, abrupt chords

4. In measure 316 begins a fugal subject derived from

    a. Motive A
    b. Motive B
    c. Theme II

5. The accompaniment in the measures immediately following measure 316 is derived from

    a. Motive A
    b. Motive B
    c. Theme IA
    d. Theme IB
    e. Theme II

6. Measures 342–347 are related to measures 316–321 by

    a. sequence
    b. augmentation
    c. diminution
    d. inversion

Béla Bartók

Concerto for Orchestra

First Movement: Sonata-allegro form

Benjamin Britten

(b. 1913)

The Young Person's Guide to the Orchestra: Variations and Fugue on a Theme of Purcell

Composed for an educational motion picture in 1946, this work has been described as "an impudently ingenious demonstration of orchestral timbres [tone colors] that is also impeccable as serious music." Through this piece—in which a narrator keeps the listener informed about what is to happen as the instruments are introduced in turn—untold thousands of students have learned to recognize the sounds of the individual instruments and of the sections of the orchestra.

No line score is given for this work, since a commentary is provided on the recording. Concentrate on the tone colors of the instruments and test your ability to recognize them by means of the questions below.

Questions for Self-Testing

1. Three woodwinds usually present in the full modern orchestra are omitted from this demonstration. They are _____, _____, and _____ .

2. In the variation featuring the violins, a rhythmic and harmonic accompaniment is provided by
   a. brasses
   b. woodwinds
   c. harp

3. As the trumpets are introduced, the prominent accompanying percussion instrument is
   a. timpani
   b. snare drum
   c. gong

4. The fugue subject is presented first in the woodwinds. The order in which they appear is
   a. flute, oboe, bassoon
   b. piccolo, bassoon, clarinet
   c. clarinet, flute, bassoon
   d. piccolo, flute, oboe

5. When the brass enter with the subject, the order is
   a. French horn, trumpet, trombone
   b. tuba, trumpet, French horn
   c. trombone, trumpet, French horn
   d. French horn, trombone, tuba

Edgar Varèse
(1885–1965)

Electronic Poem

Fascinated with the acoustical properties of sound and regarding music to be "organized sound," Varèse composed music that drew forth new sonorities from traditional vocal and instrumental resources and from new sound-producing agents. It was inevitable that he would turn to composing directly on the magnetic tape of a tape recorder, where durations can be controlled to a microsecond, dynamics fixed to a fraction of a decibel, pitches set in cycles per second, tone colors adjusted by filtering, and all other parameters fixed in the act of composing and not subject to error or "interpretation" by a performer.

This work was composed for performance at the World's Fair in Brussels in 1958 in a special pavilion equipped with some four hundred loudspeakers. The composition consists of 480 seconds of a three-track stereo tape of machine noises, transposed piano chords and bells, filtered recordings of vocalists and choruses, sinusoidal sounds produced by oscillators, and mixtures of all these.

In the pavilion it was performed with lighting effects and motion pictures. The pavilion has since been destroyed, but the music of the poem endures in a binaural stereo recorded disc.

Questions for Self-Testing

1. The initial sounds of the piece resemble

    a. gongs
    b. human voices
    c. sirens

2. Of some importance in the piece is a recurrent

    a. low note sung by a bass
    b. rhythmic hand-clapping
    c. trombone-like ascending motive

3. Toward the end of the piece, there are sounds resembling those of a jet airplane followed by a crescendo of sirens followed by

    a. the sound of an explosion
    b. the sounds of gunfire
    c. a shattering silence

Anonymous

(20th century)

Concerto Grosso for Class Impromptu

Composed in 1971 especially for this publication, this work is indicative of a trend in avant-garde music. Reacting against the total control exerted by composers of serial music and of music recorded directly by the composer on magnetic tape, some composers have turned to forms of expression of great freedom and spontaneity in which many of the events are controlled by the performers. Presumably no two performances would ever be alike.

From his experience with prepublication performances, the composer suggests that the best results are obtained when the performance is recorded on tape for immediate playback. Lacking a tape recorder, the Starter-Stopper should start and stop the piece by giving a pre-arranged signal to the performers.

Anonymous

Concerto Grosso for Class Impromptu (1971)

Full Score

PEOPLEMENTATION

Starter-Stopper—the person in charge

Concertino—no fewer than three and no more than six of the following, selected by the Starter-Stopper and positioned prominently: Piano-string Scraperplucker, Pencilsharpenerer, Lightswitcher, Chalkboardfingernailer, Wastebasketeer, Faucetfiddler, Eraserbeater, Moanerscreamergroanersinger, Shoeshuffler

Ripieno—the remaining members of the class, each of whom selects his own mode of expression, changing freely from mode to mode at any time: Hissers, Whistlers, Gigglers, Laughers, Gumpoppers, Tonguecluckers, Teethclackers, Thighslappers, Handclappers, Combthumbers, Coinrattlers, Keyringjanglers, Purseshakers, Ballpointpenclickers, Knucklepoppers, Papertearers, Spiralnotebookstrummers, Bookbangers

Continuo—Inhalers, Exhalers, Sniffers, Coughers, Sneezers, and Inescapable Environmental Noises

SECTION ONE

THEME: war
BEGINNING: when *Starter-Stopper* starts tape recorder
EVENTS: *full peoplementation* freely expresses theme
DURATION: until *ripieno* becomes silent

SECTION TWO

THEME: peace
EVENTS: *concertino* and *continuo* freely express theme; *ripieno* is silent
DURATION: until *ripieno* takes up theme of section three

SECTION THREE

THEME: love
EVENTS: *ripieno* and *continuo* freely express theme
DURATION: until *concertino* recapitulates peace theme

CODA

EVENTS: *full peoplementation* freely expresses themes of love and peace
DURATION: until everyone is suddenly aware that the piece has ended or until the *Starter-Stopper* stops the piece by turning the tape recorder off

Answers to Questions for Self-Testing

Gregorian Chant

1. b, d
2. d
3. *Agnus Dei, qui tollis peccata mundi: miserere nobis.*
   Agnus Dei, qui tollis peccata mundi: miserere nobis.
   Agnus Dei, qui tollis peccata mundi: dona nobis pacem.
4. c
5. b
6. a
7. a

Palestrina

1. 6, 11, 19, 25, 32
2. 6, 25
3. c

Purcell

1. b
2. d, e
3. b
4. b
5. 10, 14, 22, 25, 30
6. drooping
7. c
8. scatter
9. never

Bach   Brandenburg Concerto

1. b, c
2. a
3. c
4. a
5. a, c
6. b
7. b
8. oboe, oboe, flute, violin, a
9. c

Bach   Fugue

1. b
2. c
3. c
4. b

Bach   "Crucifixus"

1. 13
2. 51
3. *passus est*
4. An organ is the usual instrument.
5. a

Mozart   Figaro

1. c
2. b
3. b

Mozart   Symphony

1. a
2. a, b
3. a
4. b
5. c
6. c
7. a
8. c

Haydn   Symphony

1. a
2. c
3. c
4. a
5. c

Haydn   Quartet

1. c
2. c
3. a
4. a
5. a
6. a
7. c
8. 69

Beethoven   Sonata

1. b
2. b
3. a
4. 207
5. b
6. a
7. b

Beethoven   Symphony

1. all
2. c
3. c
4. a
5. b
6. b
7. d
8. b, c
9. a
10. b
11. c

Schubert

1. b
2. b
3. a

Chopin

1. c
2. b (in most recordings)
3. 5

Wagner

1. c
2. b
3. a
4. a
5. b
6. c

Verdi

1. c
2. a
3. b
4. c

Tchaikovsky

1. organ
2. c
3. 143–147
4. a
5. c
6. c

Brahms

1. c
2. b
3. a
4. b
5. a
6. c
7. a

Ives

1. c
2. c
3. a
4. b
5. a

Dvořák

1. a, b
2. c
3. a
4. c
5. b
6. c
7. a
8. a
9. b
10. b

Debussy

1. c
2. c
3. c
4. c

Stravinsky   Rite

1. c
2. a
3. a
4. b
5. b
6. c

Stravinsky   Octet

1. a
2. a
3. b
4. c
5. c
6. b

Webern

1. b
2. c
3. b

Bartók

1. a
2. c
3. c
4. a
5. c
6. d

Britten

1. English horn, bass clarinet, double bassoon
2. a
3. b
4. d
5. a

Varèse

1. a
2. c
3. c

Index

A   1
B   2
C   3
D   4
E   5
F   6
G   7
H   8
I   9
J   0